ANIMAL LIFE CYCLES

Penguin

by Rebecca Sabelko

BLASTOFF! READERS 2

BELLWETHER MEDIA • MINNEAPOLIS, MN

Blastoff! Readers are carefully developed by literacy experts to build reading stamina and move students toward fluency by combining standards-based content with developmentally appropriate text.

 Level 1 provides the most support through repetition of high-frequency words, light text, predictable sentence patterns, and strong visual support.

 Level 2 offers early readers a bit more challenge through varied sentences, increased text load, and text-supportive special features.

 Level 3 advances early-fluent readers toward fluency through increased text load, less reliance on photos, advancing concepts, longer sentences, and more complex special features.

★ **Blastoff! Universe**

Reading Level

Grade
K

Grades
1–3

Grade
4

This edition first published in 2021 by Bellwether Media, Inc.

No part of this publication may be reproduced in whole or in part without written permission of the publisher. For information regarding permission, write to Bellwether Media, Inc., Attention: Permissions Department, 6012 Blue Circle Drive, Minnetonka, MN 55343.

Library of Congress Cataloging-in-Publication Data

Names: Sabelko, Rebecca, author.
Title: Penguin / by Rebecca Sabelko.
Description: Minneapolis : Bellwether Media, 2021. | Series: Blastoff! reader : Animal life cycles | Includes bibliographical references and index. | Audience: Ages 5-8 | Audience: Grades K-1 | Summary: "Relevant images match informative text in this introduction to the life cycle of a penguin. Intended for students in kindergarten through third grade"-- Provided by publisher.
Identifiers: LCCN 2020036819 (print) | LCCN 2020036820 (ebook) | ISBN 9781644874110 (library binding) | ISBN 9781648340888 (ebook)
Subjects: LCSH: Penguins--Life cycles--Juvenile literature.
Classification: LCC QL696.S47 S23 2021 (print) | LCC QL696.S47 (ebook) | DDC 598.47156--dc23
LC record available at https://lccn.loc.gov/2020036819
LC ebook record available at https://lccn.loc.gov/2020036820

Editor: Betsy Rathburn   Designer: Jeffrey Kollock

Printed in the United States of America, North Mankato, MN.

Table of **Contents**

Penguins are flightless birds.
They spend most of their
time swimming in the sea.

All penguins live in the southern **hemisphere**. They gather in **colonies** to raise their young.

colony

Life Cycle of a Penguin

The penguin life cycle begins when females lay one or two eggs.

Penguin parents keep the eggs safe and warm. Most take turns. They tuck their eggs into their **brood pouches**.

brood pouch

After one or two months, the **chicks** use an **egg tooth** to break out of their shells.

egg
tooth

chick

It takes about two days to **hatch**!

The helpless chicks are covered in fuzzy **down**. They are very hungry!

Penguin Diet

Chick

regurgitated fish

Fledgling

small fish

Adult

small fish

krill

down

Most chicks eat **regurgitated** fish from their parents' mouths.

The chicks grow fast. But they need help to stay warm.

They tuck under their parents' bodies. They only peek their heads out to eat.

Soon, the chicks
need more food.
Both parents must
leave to hunt.

The chicks join a
crèche to stay warm.
Crèches also keep
the chicks safe.

crèche

molting

In a few months, the chicks **molt** their down. They grow **waterproof** feathers.

Growing Up: Emperor Penguin

Egg		up to **75** days
Chick		around **5** months
Fledgling		around **5** years
Adult		**15** to **20** years

The chicks are now **fledglings**. They are ready for life in the sea!

Fledglings spend up to eight years at sea. They grow into adults.

The adults return to where they were born. It is time to find a **mate**!

Emperor Penguin Growth

Egg

up to 1 pound
(0.5 kilograms)

Chick

up to 0.4 pounds
(0.2 kilograms)

Fledgling

around 50 pounds
(23 kilograms)

Adult

up to 100 pounds
(45 kilograms)

After mating, female
penguins lay eggs.
Time for new life to begin!

Life Cycle of a Penguin

1.

Egg

2.

Chick

3.

Fledgling

4.

Adult

Glossary

brood pouches—warm layers of skin where penguins keep their eggs

chicks—baby penguins

colonies—large groups of penguins that live together

crèche—a group of young penguins gathered together to stay safe and warm

down—small, soft feathers that cover a penguin chick's body

egg tooth—a sharp bump on the top of a penguin chick's beak

fledglings—young penguins that have feathers that allow them to swim

hatch—to break out of an egg

hemisphere—a half of the Earth

mate—a partner

molt—to shed fur or skin for growth

regurgitated—brought up from the stomach

waterproof—able to keep water from passing through

To Learn More

AT THE LIBRARY

Adamson, Heather. *Emperor Penguins*. Minneapolis, Minn.: Bellwether Media, 2018.

Boyer, Crispin. *So Cute! Penguins*. Washington, D.C.: National Geographic Kids, 2020.

Gray, Susan H. *Emperor Penguin Migration*. Ann Arbor, Mich.: Cherry Lake Publishing, 2021.

ON THE WEB

FACTSURFER

Factsurfer.com gives you a safe, fun way to find more information.

1. Go to www.factsurfer.com.

2. Enter "penguin" into the search box and click 🔍.

3. Select your book cover to see a list of related content.

Index

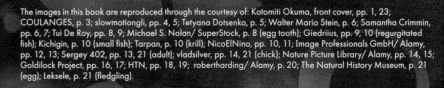

The images in this book are reproduced through the courtesy of: Kotomiti Okuma, front cover, pp. 1, 23; COULANGES, p. 3; slowmotiongli, pp. 4, 5; Tetyana Dotsenko, p. 5; Walter Mario Stein, p. 6; Samantha Crimmin, pp. 6, 7; Tui De Roy, pp. 8, 9; Michael S. Nolan/ SuperStock, p. 8 (egg tooth); Giedriius, pp. 9, 10 (regurgitated fish); Kichigin, p. 10 (small fish); Tarpan, p. 10 (krill); NicoElNino, pp. 10, 11; Image Professionals GmbH/ Alamy, pp. 12, 13; Sergey 402, pp. 13, 21 (adult); vladsilver, pp. 14, 21 (chick); Nature Picture Library/ Alamy, pp. 14, 15; Goldilock Project, pp. 16, 17; HTN, pp. 18, 19; robertharding/ Alamy, p. 20; The Natural History Museum, p. 21 (egg); Leksele, p. 21 (fledgling).